1824

# Josefina's Cook Book

*A Peek at
Dining in the
Past with Meals
You Can Cook Today*

PLEASANT COMPANY PUBLICATIONS

Printed in the United States of America.
98 99 00 01 02 03 04 WCR 10 9 8 7 6 5 4 3 2 1

The American Girls Collection®, Josefina®, and Josefina Montoya™ are trademarks of Pleasant Company.

PICTURE CREDITS
The following individuals and organizations have generously given permission to reprint images in this book:
Page 1—Corbis; 2—Jack Parsons Photography; 3—Alexander Harmer, History Collections, Los Angeles
County Museum of Natural History (top); Courtesy Museum of New Mexico, neg. #3712 (bottom right);
5—Renée Comet Photography, Inc., © 1996; 7—Photo by Andy King, courtesy Lerner Publications (bottom
left); Museum of International Folk Art, Museum of New Mexico, Santa Fe. Photo by Blair Clark (bottom
right); 9—Artifacts from the Marc Simmons Collection; 13—Photo by James N. Furlong, courtesy Museum of
New Mexico, neg. #138858; 14—Courtesy Mondadori; 15—Leonhard Ferdinand Meisner, ...de cafe, chocolatae
herbae thee ac nicotianae; 16—School of American Research Collections at the Museum of International Folk Art,
Museum of New Mexico, Santa Fe. Photo by Blair Clark; 17—Photo by SCS, Selgem #87.45.493, courtesy
Maxwell Museum of Anthropology, University of New Mexico, Albuquerque; 19—Wangensteen Historical
Library of Biology and Medicine, Biomedical Library (top); Courtesy University of Pennsylvania Museum
(bottom); 21—Corbis-Bettmann (top); Courtesy Mondadori (bottom); 22—Edward S. Curtis, Library of
Congress; 29—Courtesy Museum of New Mexico, neg. #58874; 30—Courtesy Mondadori; 32—From The Art of
Mexican Cooking, © 1989 by Diana Kennedy. Used by permission of Bantam Books, a division of Bantam
Doubleday Dell Publishing Group, Inc.; Hauberg Indian Museum (right); 33—Courtesy Mondadori; 35—Jack
Parsons Photography; 39—Photo © 1992 Tom Wallis; 41—Wangensteen Historical Library of Biology and
Medicine, Biomedical Library; 42—Nuestra Señora de los Dolores/Our Lady of Sorrows, Arroyo Hondo Carver,
Museum of International Folk Art, Museum of New Mexico, Santa Fe. Photo by Blair Clark (left); Santa Inez/St.
Agnes, attributed to Pedro Antonio Fresquis, Spanish Colonial Arts Society, Inc. Collection on loan to the
Museum of International Folk Art, Museum of New Mexico, Santa Fe. Photo by Blair Clark (right); 43—Photo
by Edwin S. Andrews, courtesy Museum of New Mexico, neg. #71218; 44—Alexander Harmer, History
Collections, Los Angeles County Museum of Natural History.

Written and Edited by Tamara England
Designed and Art Directed by Pat Tuchscherer and Jane S. Varda
Produced by Virginia Gunderson, Cheryll Mellenthin, and Anne Ruh
Cover Illustration by Mike Wimmer
Inside Illustrations by Susan McAliley
Photography by Mark Salisbury
Historical and Picture Research by Rebecca Sample Bernstein,
Kathy Borkowski, Tamara England, and Debra Shapiro
Recipe Testing Coordinated by Jean doPico
Food Styling by Janice Bell
Prop Research by Jean doPico

Special thanks to Sandra Jaramillo, Tey Diana Rebolledo, Orlando Romero,
and Marc Simmons for their review of the manuscript.

**Library of Congress Cataloging-in-Publication Data**

Josefina's cookbook : a peek at dining in the past with meals you can cook today /
[written and edited by Tamara England ; inside illustrations by Susan McAliley ;
photography by Mark Salisbury]. — 1st ed.
p. cm. — (The American girls collection)
Summary: Information about the foods, cooking, kitchens, and dining customs
of the people who lived in northern New Mexico in 1824 and whose culture combined
Spanish, Mexican, and Native American traditions.
ISBN 1-56247-669-6 (softcover)
1. Mexican American cookery—Juvenile literature. 2. Cookery—New Mexico—Juvenile literature.
3. New Mexico—Social life and customs—19th century—Juvenile literature. [1. Mexican American cookery.
2. Cookery—New Mexico. 3. New Mexico—Social life and customs—19th century.]
I. England, Tamara. II. McAliley, Susan, ill. III. Salisbury, Mark, ill. IV. Series.
TX715.2.S69J67 1998 641.5972—dc21 98-4745 CIP AC

# Contents

S pecial thanks to all the children and adults who tested the recipes and gave us their valuable comments:

Emerald Abel and her mother Dolly Marie Torres
Maggie Airriess and her mother Sandra Beaupré
Amy Albanese and her mother Ladonna Albanese
Kelsey and Jessica Aleckson and their mother Mary Aleckson
Brittany Alioto and her mother Laurie Alioto
Laurie Barman and her mother Mary Barman
Amanda Baum and her mother Staci Baum
Karen Bednar and her mother Mary Bednar
Ora Ben-Ami and her mother Sara Ben-Ami
Alicia Bernards and her mother Sylvia Bernards
Kinsey Bice and her mother Pat Bice
Kensey Bille and her parents Katie and Dale Bille
Ashley Biser and her mother Chris Biser
Sarah Bly and her mother Jeanine Bly
Mary Jo Bohlman and her mother Joan Bohlman
Audra and Anne Brady and their mother Pat Brady
Lindsay Brooks and her mother Elizabeth Brooks
Molly Brosius and her mother Mary Brosius
Kathleen Cash and her mother Barb Cash
Alanna Clarke and her mother Mary Anne Clarke
Annie Clayton and her mother Barbara Clayton
Ali Close and her mother Pam Close
Annie Cohen and her mother Liz Cohen
Katelyn Collien and her mother Beth Collien
Ginnette Counselman and her mother Sue Counselman
Anna-Lisa Dahlgren and her mother Donna Dahlgren
Rose Dauck and her mother Linda Dauck
Mimi Davis and her mother Lindy Davis
Katie Debs and her mother Andrea Debs
Catherine Degen and her mother Eve Degen
Lindsey Dieter and her mother Debbie Dieter
Genieve Dodsworth and her mother Beth Dodsworth
Ella Joyce and her mother Ann Joyce
Chelsey Karns and her mother Karen Karns
Clare Kazanski and her mother Madelyn Leopold
Katie Martinez and her mother Deborah Martinez
Rachel and Emily Meyer and their mother Ruth Meyer
Maggie Rodgers and her mother Anne Rodgers
Kristina Roybal and her mother Anna Roybal

# COOKING IN NEW MEXICO

I n the 1820s, families on northern New Mexico *ranchos*, or farms, grew most of their own food. While the men and boys worked in the fields and tended the animals, women and girls like Josefina Montoya and her sisters tended the gardens, cooked, and preserved food for the winter.

Like the Pueblo Indians who had lived there for many hundreds of years, the Spanish and Mexican settlers who arrived in the 1600s and 1700s grew corn, beans, and squash. These foods, along with many varieties of *chiles*, were the **staples**, or basic foods, of New Mexican cooking. A girl like Josefina learned many ways to prepare corn— fresh, dried, roasted, treated with lime, and ground into cornmeal flour. But New Mexican cooks served other foods, too. They made fresh cheese from goat's milk and collected eggs from their own chickens. Meat came from their herds of goats and sheep, as well as from wild deer, buffalo, and rabbits that were hunted or trapped.

Special foods, such as sugar and chocolate, and spices like cinnamon and anise seed came all the way from Mexico City—a journey that could take as long as four or five months. The arrival of traders with goods from southern Mexico was the perfect occasion to prepare a special feast to share with friends and neighbors.

Learning about kitchens and cooking in the past will help you understand what it was like to grow up the way Josefina did. Cooking the foods she ate will bring history alive for you and your family today.

### JOSEFINA ✳ 1824

*María Josefina Montoya lived in northern New Mexico in 1824, when it was still part of Mexico. Josefina and her sisters grew up learning to cook foods that combined Spanish, Mexican, and Native American traditions.*

●

*Remember that in Spanish, "j" is pronounced like "h." That means that Josefina's name is pronounced "ho-seh-FEE-nah."*

# GLOSSARY OF SPANISH WORDS

## THE RANCHO

*Josefina and her family lived on a **rancho**, or farm. The Montoyas raised most of their own food in the fields, gardens, and orchards around their home, and got water from the nearby stream. The rancho house had thick walls made of **adobe** bricks and plaster that surrounded an inside courtyard. The thick walls kept them cool in summer and warm in winter.*

## CHILE RISTRAS

*Women and children preserved ripe **chiles** for the winter by hanging them in strings, or **ristras**, to dry. They tied the stems together with string made from the twisted fibers of the yucca plant.*

You'll find some Spanish words in this book. Use this glossary if you can't tell what a word means or how to pronounce it.

**acequia** *(ah-SEH-kee-ah)*—an irrigation ditch

**adobe** *(ah-DOH-beh)*—a building material made of earth and straw

**bizcochito** *(bees-ko-CHEE-toh)*—a kind of sugar cookie

**calabacita** *(kah-lah-bah-SEE-tah)*—a squash

**Camino Real** *(kah-MEE-no rey-AHL)*—the main trail from Mexico City to New Mexico

**carne adovada** *(KAR-neh ah-doh-VAH-dah)*—meat in a red chile sauce

**chile** *(CHEE-leh)*—the fruit of chile plants; also sometimes called a pepper

**cocina** *(ko-SEE-nah)*—a kitchen; also, cooking

**empanadita** *(em-pah-nah-DEE-tah)*—a small pie or tart filled with fruit, nuts, or meat

**fandango** *(fahn-DAHN-go)*—a lively dance party

**frijoles** *(free-HO-les)*—beans

**horno** *(OR-no)*—an outdoor oven made of adobe

**mano** *(MAH-no)*—a stone held in the hand and used to grind food on a flat stone *metate*

**masa harina** *(MAH-sah ah-REE-nah)*—cornmeal flour

**metate** *(meh-TAH-teh)*—a large flat stone used with a *mano* to grind corn, chiles, or other foods

**molinillo** *(mo-lee-NEE-yo)*—a wooden utensil for stirring hot chocolate

**piloncillo** *(pee-lohn-SEE-yo)*—a sugar cone

**posole** *(po-SO-leh)*—hominy, or preserved corn

**quelites** *(keh-LEE-tes)*—a green plant called lambs' quarters in English

**rancho** *(RAHN-cho)*—a farm or ranch

**ristra** *(REE-strah)*—a string of chiles

**sopaipilla** *(so-pah-PEE-yah)*—a fried bread puff

**tamales** *(tah-MAH-les)*—spicy meat surrounded by cornmeal dough and cooked in a cornhusk wrapping

**torreja** *(toh-REH-hah)*—puffed egg fritter

**tortilla** *(tor-TEE-yah)*—a kind of flat, round bread

# RANCHO KITCHENS

Josefina's *cocina*, or kitchen, did not look much like your kitchen today. There was no sink with running water and no refrigerator to keep things cool. The oven, or *horno*, was outside in the courtyard. In one corner of the kitchen, a fire burned most of the day in an open hearth. Above the hearth was a **shepherd's bed**, a ledge where shepherds slept when they had orphaned lambs to keep warm, and where foods were sometimes dried.

The floor was dirt mixed with ox blood, which hardened the dirt and made the floor easier to keep clean. Every day, the sisters swept the dirt floor with grass brooms dipped in water to "lay the dust."

All around the kitchen hung dried herbs, fruits, chiles, and vegetables. Other foods, such

as wheat, corn, and dried meats, were kept in dark storage rooms next to the kitchen. Carmen, the cook, put things that needed to be kept cool, such as fresh cheese, in a small closed cupboard built into the thick adobe wall.

A large pottery jar held water from the stream for cooking and cleaning. Smaller pottery bean pots and baskets sat on open wooden shelves, with hand-carved wooden spoons and gourd ladles hanging below. A few iron pots and tools from Mexico City sat beside the hearth. The Montoyas' special silver cups and dishes and silverware were stored in a locked wooden cupboard.

## MANO AND METATE

*Every household in New Mexico had at least one **mano** and **metate** for grinding corn, chiles, and other foods. Women and girls sometimes spent several hours every day just grinding corn!*

## HORNOS

*Cooks in Josefina's time did their baking outside in large adobe ovens called **hornos**. To heat the horno, a wood fire was built inside the oven. After the wood had turned to coals and heated the horno to just the right temperature, all the coals were removed. Then the inside was wiped clean with a damp cloth, and the food was sealed inside to cook. Hornos were used for baking bread and pies, roasting corn and chiles, and cooking stews.*

# TIPS FOR TODAY'S COOKS

### MEASURING FLOUR

*A good cook measures exactly. Here is a hint for measuring flour. Spoon the flour into a measuring cup, heaping it up over the top. Then use the spoon handle to level off the flour. Don't shake or tap the cup.*

### TABLE OF MEASUREMENTS

3 teaspoons = 1 tablespoon
2 cups = 1 pint
2 pints = 1 quart
4 cups = 1 quart

You'll find below a list of things that every good cook should know. But this is the most important tip: **work with an adult.** This is the safe way for you to work in the kitchen. Cooking together is fun, too. It's a tradition American families have always shared. Keep it alive today!

**1.** Choose a time that suits you and the adult who's cooking with you, so that you will both enjoy working together in the kitchen.

**2.** Wash your hands with soap before and after you handle food. Wear an apron, tie back your hair, and roll up your sleeves.

**3.** Read a recipe carefully, all the way through, before you start it. Look at the pictures. They will help you understand the steps.

**4.** Gather all the ingredients and equipment you will need before you start to cook. Put everything where you can reach it easily.

**5.** Ask an adult to show you how to peel, cut, and grate with sharp kitchen tools. Always use a chopping board to save kitchen counters.

**6.** Pay attention while using knives so that you don't cut your fingers! Remember—a good, sharp knife is safer than a dull one.

**7.** When you stir or mix, hold the bowl or pan steady on a flat surface, not in your arms.

8. Make sure your mixing bowls, pots, and pans are the right size. If they are too small, you'll probably spill. If pots and pans are too large, foods will burn more easily.

9. Clean up spills right away.

10. Pots and pans will be less likely to spill on the stove if you turn the handles toward the side.

11. Have an adult handle hot pans. Don't use the stove burners or the oven without permission or supervision.

12. Turn off the burner or the oven as soon as a dish is cooked.

13. Potholders and oven mitts will protect you from burns. Use them when you touch anything hot. Protect kitchen counters by putting trivets or cooling racks under hot pots and pans.

14. Keep hot foods hot and cold foods cold. If you plan to make things early and serve them later, store them properly. Foods that could spoil belong in the refrigerator. Wrap foods well.

15. If you decide to make a whole meal, be sure to plan so that all the food will be ready when you are ready to serve it.

16. Cleanup is part of cooking, too. Leave the kitchen at least as clean as you found it. Wash all the dishes, pots, and pans. Sweep the floor. Throw away the garbage.

## COOKING WITH CHILES

❋ *The recipes in this cookbook use ground, or powdered, chiles. When a recipe calls for ground chiles, do **not** use commercial "chili powder"—it's not the same!*

❋ *Not all chiles are hot. You can find mild ground red or ancho chiles at spice shops, natural foods stores, or Mexican grocery stores.*

❋ *When working with chiles—even mild chiles—never touch your eyes without first washing your hands well! The oils in the chiles can burn your eyes.*

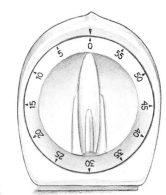

## TIMING

*When a recipe gives two cooking times— for example, when it says, "bake 25 to 30 minutes"—first set the timer for the shorter time. If the food is not done when the timer rings, give it more time.*

# BREAKFAST

*Carmen started the morning fire with a curved iron tool called a "strike-a-light." By hitting it against a piece of flint, she made a spark to light the fire.*

Josefina loved the sounds of the morning. In summer, she awoke at first light, when birds chirped in the orchard and the animals stirred in their pens. But on dark winter mornings, she was awakened by the sound of Carmen, the cook, slip-slapping *tortillas* into shape in the kitchen. Every morning, while the rest of the household slept, Carmen got up early and started the family's breakfast.

Josefina dressed quickly and hurried to the kitchen. The cozy room was especially welcoming on cold mornings. There was always a fire in the open hearth in the corner. The air was rich with the smells of herbs and chiles that hung from the beams. Josefina liked to warm up in front of the fire before taking a large pottery jar to the stream to get water for cooking, drinking, and cleaning. Sometimes Carmen let Josefina make herself a tortilla to eat on her way to the stream.

By the time Josefina returned with the water jar carefully balanced on her head, her sisters had joined Carmen in the kitchen. Ana sent Josefina back outside to gather eggs for the *torrejas*, or egg fritters, that Papá liked so much. Clara cooked tortillas on the iron griddle by the fire. Francisca unwrapped the soft goat cheese she had made the day before.

On feast days or other special occasions, the Montoyas sometimes had hot chocolate with their breakfast. First, Josefina shaved part of a cake of hard chocolate into hot water. Then, with a wooden whisk, she whipped the steamy chocolate until it was frothy and light. For a finishing touch, she sprinkled a bit of spicy cinnamon on top.

The sisters worked until the village bell called them to prayers at seven o'clock. Then, after Papá lead the family in prayer at the small altar in their home, they quickly finished their breakfast preparations, and it was time to eat!

*New Mexican cooks used a special wooden stirrer called a **molinillo** to make hot chocolate frothy.*

## BREAKFAST

❊

Flour Tortillas

•

Torrejas

•

Soft Cheese

•

Hot Chocolate

### HANDMADE BOWLS

*New Mexican kitchens did not have a lot of dishes and fancy equipment. Most things were handmade, such as this hand-carved wooden bowl.*

# FLOUR TORTILLAS

A tortilla is a flat, round bread made of cornmeal or wheat flour.

## INGREDIENTS

2 cups unbleached
  wheat flour
1/2 teaspoon salt
1/2 teaspoon baking
  powder
1/4 cup lard or
  vegetable shortening
1/2 cup hot water
Extra flour

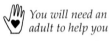 You will need an adult to help you

## EQUIPMENT

Measuring cups
  and spoons
Sifter
Large mixing bowl
Pastry cutter or fork
Wooden spoon
2 kitchen towels
Table knife
Rolling pin
Griddle or large skillet
Spatula
Potholders

## DIRECTIONS          *12 tortillas*

Step 1

Step 4

**1.** Sift together the flour, salt, and baking powder into the large mixing bowl.

**2.** Add the lard or shortening. Use the pastry cutter or fork to blend the lard and flour mixture until it becomes crumbly, like coarse sand.

**3.** Add the hot water and stir until the mixture forms a soft, sticky dough. Form the dough into a ball with your hands.

**4.** Put the dough on a surface that has been sprinkled with flour. Dust your hands with flour and knead the dough for about 1 minute. To knead the dough, press down on it with the heels of your hands. Then fold it in half. Press it and fold it again. Add a little more flour if the dough sticks.

5. Cover the dough with a damp towel and set it aside for about 10 minutes.

6. Flatten the dough slightly, then cut it into 12 equal pieces. First cut the dough in half. Then cut each half in half again (into quarters). Finally, cut each quarter into 3 pieces.

**MEASURING BOXES**

*Papá measured crops such as wheat, corn, and beans in boxes like these. But even with measuring boxes, measurements weren't always exact. That's because some crops were measured even with the top of the box, while others were measured heaping. How a crop was measured sometimes changed from one community to the next.*

7. Form each piece into a ball. Set the dough balls aside, covered with the damp towel, for 30 minutes. This allows the dough to "relax" so it will stretch better when you roll it out.

8. Sprinkle flour on your work surface, the rolling pin, your hands, and the dough balls.

9. To make a tortilla, flatten 1 dough ball with the heel of your hand. Roll the ball into a circle, 1/8 to 1/4 inch thick and 6 to 7 inches across.

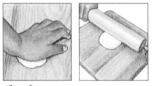

*Step 9*

10. Heat the griddle over medium-high heat for 5 minutes. Have an adult help you put the tortilla on the griddle, using the spatula or your fingers. Cook it for about 30 seconds, until it has light brown spots on the bottom.

11. Use the spatula to gently turn over the tortilla. Within 15 to 20 seconds, it will puff up and turn brown in spots. Cook it until the dough dries a little and looks slightly wrinkled, but is still soft and flexible.

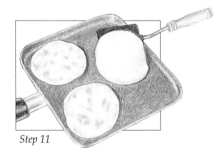

*Step 11*

12. Wrap the cooked tortillas in a dry towel so they stay soft until you serve them. ✳

# TORREJAS

*Torrejas are fluffy egg fritters that puff up
in the pan and then melt in your mouth!*

## INGREDIENTS

Corn oil or vegetable oil
3 eggs
3 tablespoons flour
¼ teaspoon baking
    powder
⅛ teaspoon or less salt
Red chile sauce, page 20
*(optional)*

*You will need an
adult to help you*

## EQUIPMENT

Deep-fat fryer or deep,
    heavy skillet or pan
Cooking thermometer
Paper towels
Medium mixing bowl
Small mixing bowl
Table fork
Measuring cups
    and spoons
Electric mixer
Wooden spoon
Tablespoon
Slotted spoon
Potholders

## DIRECTIONS          *15 to 20 fritters*

Step 1

**1.** Pour the oil into the fryer or skillet. Clip the
thermometer to the edge. Position it so the tip
of the thermometer is in the oil but does not
touch the bottom or sides of the pan. Lay
a pile of 6 paper towels on the counter.

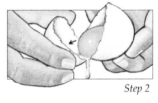

Step 2

**2.** Have an adult help you separate the egg
whites and egg yolks, as shown. Let the whites
drop into the medium mixing bowl. Drop the
yolks into the small mixing bowl.

**3.** Stir the yolks with the fork. Add the flour,
baking powder, and salt to the yolks, and stir
it all together. Set the bowl aside.

4. Have an adult help you beat the egg whites with the electric mixer until the whites are shiny and slightly stiff—so the whites form soft peaks when you pull the beaters out.

*Step 4*

5. Use the wooden spoon to scoop about ⅓ of the beaten egg whites into the yolk mixture, and stir until the mixture is soft and fluffy.

6. Gently stir the yolk mixture into the rest of the egg whites.

7. Heat the oil. When it is 350° have an adult gently slip a mounded tablespoonful of batter into the oil. The batter will immediately puff up to about double its size.

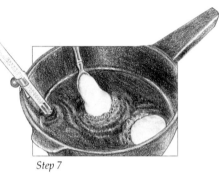

*Step 7*

8. Use the slotted spoon to turn the torreja. Fry it until it is golden brown and crisp all over.

9. Use the slotted spoon to remove the torreja, and place it on the paper towels to drain.

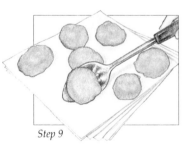

*Step 9*

10. Use the remaining batter by spoonfuls. You can cook several torrejas at a time, but don't crowd them as they cook. Be sure the oil temperature doesn't go above 375°, or the torrejas will burn.

11. Serve the torrejas immediately. You can also spoon warmed red chile sauce (page 20) over the top of the torrejas. ✽

## CHICKENS

*On a rancho like the Montoyas', goats and sheep provided meat, so chickens were more valuable for their eggs than for meat. Every day Josefina hunted for the eggs laid by their flock of speckled hens and white-faced Spanish black hens.*

# SOFT CHEESE

*New Mexican cooks often made fresh cheese first thing in the morning.*

## INGREDIENTS

4 tablets of Junket® rennet*
2 teaspoons water
½ gallon goat's milk
  (**not** *ultra-pasteurized*)
3 tablespoons plain
  yogurt with live cultures
  (**not** *low-fat or nonfat*)
1½ teaspoons salt

*Found in the baking section
of many supermarkets.

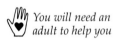 *You will need an
adult to help you*

## EQUIPMENT

Small bowl
Small spoon
Measuring spoons
Large saucepan
Large spoon
Candy or cooking
  thermometer
Colander or sieve
Cheesecloth, 2 single-layer
  pieces, each 12 to 18
  inches long
9" x 12" baking pan
Large knife
Large slotted spoon

## DIRECTIONS    *¼ to ½ pound cheese*

**1.** Put the rennet tablets in the small bowl and crush them with the back of the small spoon. Add the water, stir to dissolve, and set aside.

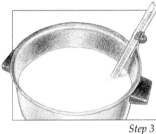
*Step 1*

**2.** Pour the milk into the large saucepan. Add the yogurt and salt, and stir to mix completely.

**3.** Clip the thermometer to the edge of the saucepan. The tip of the thermometer should not touch the bottom or sides of the saucepan.

*Step 3*

**4.** Turn on the burner to medium-high to heat the milk mixture to about 90°, or "wrist warm"—warm, but still cool enough so you can stir it with your finger.

5. Turn off the heat and move the pan from the burner to a warm spot in your kitchen. Remove the thermometer and gently stir in the dissolved rennet and water.

6. Let the saucepan stand undisturbed for at least 1 hour so it can "set," or form a thick, stiff curd. This may take several hours longer if the room is cool.

7. As the milk sets, line the colander with 2 layers of dampened cheesecloth. Place the lined colander in the baking pan.

8. When the milk has turned into a custard-like curd, use the knife to cut the curd into 2-inch chunks. Use the slotted spoon to gently move the pieces into the colander to drain.

9. Let the cheese stand at room temperature for at least 4 hours so the whey can drain. Do not stir it, but from time to time tilt the colander or sieve and adjust the cheesecloth to help drain the whey. As the pan fills with whey, pour it out so the cheese is not standing in the whey.

10. When all the whey has drained, the cheese can be gently molded with your hands into a ball.

11. Serve the cheese immediately, or store it in the refrigerator for up to a week. ❀

### GOATS' MILK

*A small herd of goats Mamá left Josefina and her sisters provided milk for the household. This herd was kept close to the rancho, where the animals could be milked daily. The rest of the rancho's goats stayed in larger herds in mountainside pastures.*

Step 7

Step 8

Step 9

### HOMEMADE RENNET

*Rennet is a chemical that makes milk form into soft curds—the first step in making cheese. Today, rennet is available in tablets. Cooks in Josefina's time could get rennet only from the lining of a young goat's stomach. Whenever a goat was butchered, a cook would carefully wash and air-dry the stomach lining, and then save it for making cheese.*

13

# HOT CHOCOLATE

*In 1824, hot chocolate was a special treat for a girl like Josefina.*

## INGREDIENTS

5 tablespoons powdered, unsweetened cocoa

1/2 teaspoon cinnamon

1/8 teaspoon ground nutmeg

Pinch of salt

1/3 cup honey

1/2 cup hot water

4 cups whole milk

1 teaspoon vanilla

## EQUIPMENT

Measuring cups and spoons

Medium saucepan

Wooden spoon

Potholders

Kitchen towel

Wire whisk, rotary beater, or a *molinillo*

*You will need an adult to help you*

## DIRECTIONS     *About 4 servings*

1. Combine the cocoa, cinnamon, nutmeg, salt, and honey in the saucepan and mix well. Stir in the hot water.

2. Turn on the burner to medium-high and stir the mixture constantly until it just begins to *boil*, or bubble rapidly. Quickly turn down the heat so the mixture barely *simmers*, or bubbles gently, for about 30 seconds. Stir constantly.

*Step 3*

3. Add the milk to the mixture in the saucepan. Stir it constantly over medium heat for 1 to 2 minutes to heat it, but do not let it boil.

4. Have an adult remove the saucepan from the burner and set it on a damp towel on a counter or table. The damp towel will help keep the saucepan steady in step 5.

5. Stir in the vanilla. Then have an adult help you hold the saucepan steady while you use the wire whisk or rotary beater to rapidly beat the hot chocolate until it is very frothy.

*Step 5*

6. Pour the frothy chocolate into mugs, and add a small sprinkling of cinnamon on top just before serving. ✳

### THE FOOD OF THE GODS

*Chocolate comes from the seeds of* **cacao** *plants. The ancient Mayas and Aztecs—the native people of Central America—considered chocolate to be the "food of the gods" because it made them feel good and gave long-lasting energy. They served it as a bitter drink flavored with vanilla and chiles. In the 1500s, the Spanish took chocolate to Europe, where it was sweetened with sugar. In Josefina's time, partly sweetened chocolate came from Mexico City in the form of hardened wafers.*

*Cacao*

### VANILLA

*Vanilla flavoring comes from the vanilla bean, and was originally used to flavor chocolate. When the Spanish brought chocolate to Spain, Europeans soon discovered that vanilla was delicious as a flavor by itself.*

# DINNER

*Families like Josefina's kept their
special dishes and silverware in
hand-carved wooden cupboards.*

Dinner at mid-day was the main meal of the day for the Montoyas. In warm weather, it was usually eaten outside in the courtyard, right after noon prayers.

Josefina and Clara had the job of arranging the serving table in the courtyard. They brought plates and cups from the wooden cupboard in the kitchen. Carmen carried out large bowls of beans and squash, or *calabacitas*. There were smaller bowls of red or green chile sauce. In spring and early summer, the family enjoyed eating *quelites*, a plant that grew wild in the hills around the rancho. And on special occasions, there was usually a special dish to enjoy, such as *carne adovada*—meat cooked in red chile sauce.

Carmen served the food with carved wooden spoons or gourd ladles, or the family used tortillas to scoop the food right from the serving bowls. A basket of warm *sopaipillas*, fried bread puffs, completed the meal. Sopaipillas puffed up as they cooked—they reminded Josefina of the way her little hen puffed up when she clucked!

The Montoyas ate sitting on benches built into the wall, or sitting on the ground. After dinner, during the hottest part of the afternoon, everyone rested. Then they went back to work in the late afternoon and evening hours.

In the cooler months, the Montoyas ate dinner inside. As the days grew cold, there was less fresh food and more preserved food on the table. Mamá had taught Josefina and her sisters all about preserving food. Drying was the most common way to preserve food—in the dry air and hot sun of New Mexico, food dried quickly. Josefina and her sisters preserved chiles by hanging them in strings, or *ristras*, to dry. They also dried pumpkins, squashes, and fruits. By preserving food in autumn, they made sure they would have good things for dinner all winter long!

**DINNER**

❋

Beans

•

Red Chile Sauce

•

Carne Adovada

•

Quelites

•

Calabacitas

•

Sopaipillas

*Drying corn and chiles*

17

# Carne Adovada

*Carne adovada is meat **marinated**, or soaked, in a red chile sauce.*

## INGREDIENTS

Vegetable or corn oil to grease baking dish
$1\frac{1}{2}$ pounds boneless pork chops or pork roast
2 cups red chile sauce *(page 20)*
Tortillas, page 8 *(optional)*

*You will need an adult to help you*

## EQUIPMENT

Medium glass or ceramic baking dish with a tight-fitting lid
Sharp knife
Cutting board
Measuring cup
Potholders
Trivet

## DIRECTIONS

***4 to 5 servings***

*Step 1*

1. Grease the baking dish with oil. Have an adult help you trim any fat from the pork and cut it into 1-to-2-inch cubes.
2. Pour enough red chile sauce into the baking dish to cover the bottom of the dish.
3. Place the pork cubes on top of the sauce. Pour the remaining sauce over the pork. There should be more sauce than meat.
4. Cover the baking dish and refrigerate overnight, to let the flavor of the sauce seep in.
5. Preheat the oven to 300°. Bake, covered, for 3 to $3\frac{1}{2}$ hours. After $2\frac{1}{2}$ hours, have an adult check to see if the meat is tender and if the sauce has cooked down. If the sauce is watery, cook uncovered for the last $\frac{1}{2}$ hour or so.
6. Have an adult place the hot baking dish on a trivet on the table, and serve with warm flour tortillas to wrap around the meat. ❉

### Wild Game

*In Josefina's time, goat and sheep were the most commonly served meats. But New Mexicans also ate buffalo, deer, turkey, and rabbit. There were no refrigerators to keep meat from spoiling. People either ate meat soon after butchering it, or preserved it by drying it in thin strips, called **jerky**, as the women above are doing.*

# QUELITES

## INGREDIENTS

2 pounds fresh spinach
1 small onion
1 tablespoon lard or oil
¼ cup chopped roasted
   green chiles
   *(½ of a 4-ounce can)*
½ teaspoon salt

*You will need an
adult to help you*

## EQUIPMENT

Colander
Sharp knife
Cutting board
Measuring cups
   and spoons
Skillet with lid
Wooden spoon
Potholders
Serving dish

*In Josefina's time, quelites were
made with a spinach-like plant called
"lamb's quarters" that grows wild
in the hills of New Mexico.*

## DIRECTIONS          *4 to 6 servings*

1. Rinse the spinach leaves in cold water, and put them in the colander to drain. Throw away brown or wilted leaves. Break or cut off and discard the stems. Set the spinach aside.

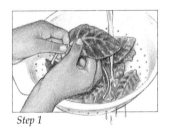
*Step 1*

2. Have an adult help you peel the onion and chop it into small pieces.

*Step 2*

3. Heat the lard or oil in the skillet over medium heat. Add the chopped onion pieces and cook them until they are lightly browned. Drain the green chiles and add to the onions. Cook, stirring constantly, for about 3 minutes.

*Step 3*

4. Add the spinach to the skillet. Stir gently until the spinach has wilted. Reduce the heat to low. Stir in the salt. Cover and cook the quelites for about 2 more minutes.

5. Have an adult help you transfer the quelites to a warmed serving dish. ❊

# CALABACITAS

Yellow and green squash, or calabacitas, made a colorful addition to Josefina's serving table.

## INGREDIENTS

4 to 6 medium zucchini or yellow summer squash
Medium onion
4 tablespoons lard or oil
½ cup chopped green chiles (1 4-ounce can)
2 cups corn kernels, fresh or frozen
½ teaspoon salt

## EQUIPMENT

Sharp knife
Cutting board
Measuring cups and spoons
Large skillet with lid
Wooden spoon
Potholders

*You will need an adult to help you*

## DIRECTIONS    *4 to 6 servings*

Step 1

**1.** Rinse the squash in cold water. Have an adult help you trim off the ends and cut the squash into ½-inch slices. Have an adult help you peel the onion and chop it into small pieces.

**2.** Heat the lard or oil in the skillet over medium heat. Add the chopped onion pieces and cook them until they are tender and clear.

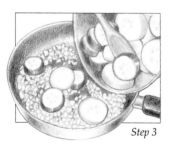

Step 3

**3.** Add the squash and stir until all the pieces are coated with oil. Cook the mixture for about 5 minutes, until the squash begins to soften.

**4.** Stir in the drained chiles, corn, and salt.

**5.** Turn the heat to low. Cover the skillet and cook everything over low heat for 15 to 20 minutes, until the squash is tender. Serve warm. ✳

# SOPAIPILLAS

## INGREDIENTS

Corn oil for deep-frying, enough for a depth of 2 inches

2 cups flour, plus extra flour for kneading

1 teaspoon salt

2 teaspoons baking powder

1 teaspoon sugar

1½ teaspoons corn oil

½ cup lukewarm water

¼ cup evaporated milk, at room temperature

Honey (optional)

*You will need an adult to help you*

## EQUIPMENT

Deep-fat fryer or deep, heavy skillet

Cooking thermometer

Paper towels

Measuring cups and spoons

Sifter

Large mixing bowl

Kitchen towel

Rolling pin

Sharp knife

Spatula

Tongs

Potholders

Napkin-lined basket

*Fluffy fried bread puffs, or sopaipillas, are fun to make!*

## DIRECTIONS     *12 sopaipillas*

**1.** Pour the corn oil into the fryer or skillet. Clip the thermometer to the edge. Position it so the tip of the thermometer is in the oil but does not touch the bottom or sides of the pan. Lay a pile of 6 paper towels on the counter.

*Step 1*

**2.** Sift together the flour, salt, baking powder, and sugar into the mixing bowl.

*Step 2*

**3.** Measure 1½ teaspoons of corn oil into the mixing bowl and mix with your fingertips until combined. Then add the lukewarm water and evaporated milk. Again use your fingertips to work the liquid into the dough until you can form a sticky ball. ➡

*Step 3*

25

## HOW TO KNEAD DOUGH

*1. Push the heels of your hands down into the dough and away from you.*

*2. Fold the dough in half.*

*3. Turn the dough.*

*4. Push the dough again. Repeat these steps. They will soon become simple, and your kneading will have a rhythm.*

**4.** Turn the dough out of the bowl onto a table or counter that has been dusted with flour. Dust your hands with flour and knead the dough for about 1 minute, until the dough is no longer sticky.

**5.** Cover the dough with a damp towel and set it aside, at room temperature, to "rest" for 15 minutes. After the dough has rested, divide it evenly into 3 balls. Cover the balls with the damp towel, and let them rest for another 20 minutes.

**6.** Sprinkle a little more flour onto the table or counter and spread it around evenly with your hands. Rub flour on your rolling pin to keep the dough from sticking.

**7.** With the rolling pin, roll out 1 ball of dough into a circle or oval until it is $1/4$ inch thick.

**8.** Use the knife to cut off any rough edges. Then cut the circle into 4 wedge-shaped pieces.

**9.** Set the pieces aside, covered with the damp towel. Don't stack them or they'll stick together!

**10.** Roll out and cut the other 2 balls of dough, and set the wedges under the damp towel with the others.

NATURAL BAKING SODA

*In Josefina's time, cooks in northern New Mexico made baking soda from a light-weight stone found in the mountains. The stones were ground into a powder to make a kind of baking soda. When cooks added water to this powder, it created a leavening that made dough rise.*

**11.** Have an adult heat the fryer or skillet until the oil is 380° to 390°. Turn the heat down a bit if it reaches 400°—do not let the oil get hot enough to smoke.

**12.** Have an adult carefully slide a wedge of dough into the hot oil. It will sink briefly into the oil, then quickly puff up and rise to the surface. After a few seconds, the top should be fully puffed up.

*Step 12*

**13.** Use the tongs to carefully turn the sopaipilla over to cook the other side. When it is light golden on both sides, use the tongs to move the sopaipilla to the paper towels to drain.

*Step 13*

**14.** Gently slide in the next wedge of dough and repeat step 13. You can fry 2 or 3 wedges at a time. Adjust the heat as needed to keep the oil a constant temperature.

**15.** Arrange the sopaipillas in a napkin-lined basket and serve them immediately. They can be served plain or with honey. ✳

### SUGAR CONES

*In Josefina's time, sugar came pressed in a hard cone shape. Cooks broke or shaved off and melted the sugar they needed. These brown-sugar cones, called* **piloncillos,** *were imported from southern Mexico. Cooks who couldn't afford imported sugar made their own corn syrup instead. You can still find piloncillos in many New Mexican groceries today.*

# FAVORITE FOODS

*Supplies from Mexico City were brought as far north as Santa Fe by traders who traveled on the **Camino Real**, or "royal road."*

When Abuelito and Tía Dolores arrived at the rancho, it was cause for celebration. Josefina was too young to dance at the *fandango*, or lively dance party, but under Ana's watchful eye, she made delicious pumpkin *empanaditas* to serve their guests. She filled each small pie with just the right amount of filling. She and Ana made the filling with pumpkins from the garden that they roasted, sweetened, and flavored with cinnamon from Mexico City.

Hospitality was important to New Mexican

families. As the oldest daughter, Ana tried hard to live up to Mamá's reputation as a gracious hostess and excellent cook. Ana made sweet *bizcochito* cookies just the way Mamá had taught her. Cooking skills and favorite recipes were handed down from mother to daughter, and now Ana and Francisca were teaching Clara and Josefina, just as Mamá had taught them.

As autumn came to New Mexico, everyone on the rancho worked extra hard to get ready for winter. Josefina looked forward to a bubbling pot of stew at the end of a long workday. Papá's favorite stew was *posole*, made with preserved corn kernels and flavored with red chiles. But Josefina preferred green chile stew—and nobody's green chile stew was better than Carmen's!

At Christmastime, Josefina and her sisters made *tamales*, spiced meat surrounded by corn-meal dough and steamed in cornhusk wrappers. Making tamales took a long time, but Josefina loved being in the kitchen with her sisters as they wrapped and tied each *tamal* in its own husk. As they worked, they told stories and sang songs that Mamá had taught them. In spite of the winter winds outside, they were warmed by working together and carrying on traditions that brought comfort and joy.

## FAVORITE FOODS

❋

Pumpkin Empanaditas

•

Posole Stew

•

Green Chile Stew

•

Bizcochitos

•

Tamales

*Acequias, or irrigation ditches, were shared by many ranchos. They carried rainwater and melting snow to fields and made it possible to farm in the dry mountains of northern New Mexico.*

# PUMPKIN EMPANADITAS

*Josefina's favorite empanaditas were stuffed with a sweet pumpkin filling.*

## NEW FOODS

*Pumpkins and squash were unknown to Spanish people before they came to America in 1492. Native Americans taught the Spanish how to cook with squash and pumpkins. Soon these vegetables became popular ingredients in Spanish recipes.*

## INGREDIENTS

**Pastry:**
2 cups flour
1 teaspoon baking powder
1/2 teaspoon salt
1/4 teaspoon cloves
1/2 teaspoon cinnamon
1/4 cup sugar
6 tablespoons lard
5 tablespoons cold
   water

**Filling:**
1 tablespoon butter
1/2 cup dark brown sugar
1 teaspoon cinnamon
1/4 teaspoon cloves
1 cup canned or fresh
   pumpkin puree

**Egg wash:**
1 egg
1 tablespoon water

## EQUIPMENT

Measuring cups
   and spoons
2 medium mixing bowls
Wooden spoon
Table knife
Pastry cutter or fork
Wax paper
1-quart saucepan
2 small bowls
Wire whisk
Rolling pin
4-inch round cookie cutter
Pastry brush
Spatula
Cookie sheets
Potholders

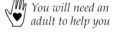 *You will need an adult to help you*

## DIRECTIONS          *12 to 16 empanaditas*

1. To make the pastry dough, measure the flour, baking powder, salt, spices, and sugar into a medium mixing bowl. Stir to mix.

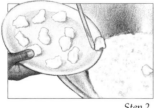
*Step 2*

2. Use the table knife to cut the lard into 12 pieces, and drop them into the flour mixture.

3. Use the pastry cutter or fork to blend the flour and lard until the mixture is crumbly.

**4.** Pour in the water and mix with a fork until the dough starts to form into a ball. Use your hands to mold the dough into a smooth ball, adding a little more water if necessary. Wrap in wax paper, and chill for 1 hour.

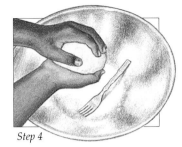
*Step 4*

**5.** To make the filling, melt the butter in the saucepan over low heat. Add the sugar, spices, and pumpkin, and stir until smooth.

**6.** Stir the filling over low heat for 10 to 15 minutes, until the mixture thickens.

**7.** Put the filling into a bowl, and let it cool a bit at room temperature. Then put it into the refrigerator, uncovered, until it is completely cold.

**8.** To make an egg wash to seal the pastry, crack the egg into a small bowl. Beat the egg with the wire whisk and stir in the water. Set it aside. Preheat the oven to 375°.

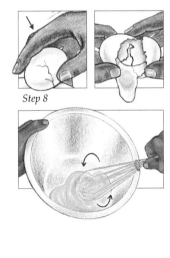
*Step 8*

**9.** Sprinkle flour onto a table and rub some on the rolling pin to keep the dough from sticking. Divide the dough into 2 balls, and wrap and refrigerate 1 ball.

**10.** Flatten the other ball slightly with your hand, then roll it from the center to the edges until it is about ¼ inch thick.

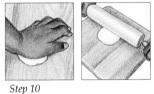
*Step 10*

**11.** Use the cookie cutter to cut as many circles as you can. ➡

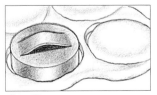
*Step 11*

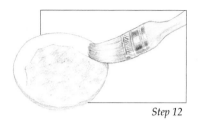

*Step 12*

**12.** Next, use the pastry brush to paint egg wash around the edge of each circle.

**13.** Put about 1 tablespoon of the filling in the center of each circle. Fold each circle in half and press the edges together with your fingers.

*Step 14*

**14.** Dip the tip of a fork in flour and press down around the edge of the empanadita.

**15.** Place the empanaditas 1 inch apart on an ungreased cookie sheet. Repeat steps 10–14 with the rest of the dough. Then brush the top of each empanadita with egg wash, and make steam vents by pricking the center of each one with the fork.

**16.** Bake the empanaditas for 15 to 20 minutes, until they are lightly browned. Have an adult remove them from the oven, then sprinkle a little sugar on each one as they cool. Let them cool quite a bit before serving, because the filling stays hot even after the crust cools. ✳

## MORTAR AND PESTLE

*New Mexican cooks ground spices like cinnamon and allspice with a mortar and pestle. A **mortar** is a small bowl made of stone or wood. Cooks used the **pestle**, a small club, to grind spices and mash herbs in the mortar.*

## PRESERVING PUMPKINS

*During the fall harvest, everyone worked together cutting and hanging pumpkins to dry in the autumn sun, as these Native Americans are doing.*

# POSOLE STEW

## INGREDIENTS

1 cup or 6–8 ounces dried *posole* corn kernels*

4 cups of water, or more

¾ pound pork roast

1 small onion

2 cloves garlic

1 teaspoon oregano

2 teaspoons salt

1 tablespoon ground red chiles, or more to taste (**not** chili powder)

## EQUIPMENT

Large mixing bowl

Colander

Measuring cups and spoons

Large saucepan with lid

Sharp knife

Cutting board

Wooden spoon

Potholders

 *You will need an adult to help you*

*Posole is a traditional stew made of hominy, or preserved corn.*

## DIRECTIONS     *About 4 servings*

1. Soak the dried posole overnight in the mixing bowl, in enough water to cover it. Then drain and rinse the posole in the colander. Put it in the saucepan, along with 4 cups of water.

2. Have an adult help you cut the pork into 1-inch cubes, and peel and chop the onion and garlic. Add it all to the saucepan, along with the oregano, salt, and ground chiles.

3. Cook on medium-high heat until the mixture starts to *boil*, or bubble rapidly. Turn the heat to medium-low and let the stew *simmer*, or bubble gently, uncovered, for 1 hour.

4. After an hour, stir and check that there is at least 1 inch of water above the posole. Add water if necessary. Then cover and let the stew simmer gently for 2 more hours, until the posole is puffed, tender, and ready to eat. ✳

*Posole can be found at Mexican grocery stores, many natural foods stores, and some large supermarkets.*

Step 2

### PRESERVING CORN

*Cooks preserved corn by boiling the kernels in water mixed with wood ash or burned limestone. This created what Native Americans called **nixtamal**—often called **hominy** today. The hard outer skin of the kernels fell away, leaving the soft inner kernel to eat whole or to grind into cornmeal flour.*

# GREEN CHILE STEW

*Green chile stew makes a satisfying meal at the end of a long day.*

## INGREDIENTS

2 pounds lean stew beef
1½ cups onion
5 cloves garlic
5 tablespoons corn oil
1 cup chopped green
    chiles *(2 4-ounce cans,
    or use fresh roasted chiles)*
2½ cups water
¾ teaspoon salt
1 tablespoon plus
    2 teaspoons flour

## EQUIPMENT

Sharp knife
Cutting board
Measuring cups
    and spoons
Large heavy skillet
    with lid
Wooden spoon
Slotted spoon
Plate
Potholders
Small skillet

*You will need an adult to help you*

***About 6 servings***

## DIRECTIONS

1. Have an adult help you cut the beef into ½-inch cubes. Set aside.

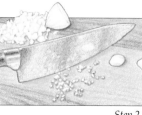
*Step 2*

2. Have an adult help you peel the onion and garlic and chop them very fine. Set aside.

3. Heat 3 tablespoons of oil in the heavy skillet over medium-high heat. When the oil starts to smoke, have an adult put the beef into the oil. Stir the beef to brown it on all sides.

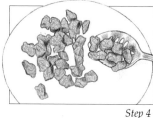
*Step 4*

4. When all the beef has browned, turn the heat down to medium and use a slotted spoon to move the beef onto a plate. Set aside.

5. Add 1 more tablespoon of oil to the skillet, along with the onions and garlic, and stir together over medium heat. Cook until the onions are soft and clear but not browned.

**6.** Drain the chiles and stir them in with the onions and garlic. Cook for about 1 minute.

*Step 6*

**7.** Put the beef back into the skillet and add the 2½ cups of water. Heat the mixture until it *boils,* or bubbles rapidly. Then turn the heat down to medium-low, cover, and cook the stew so that it *simmers,* or bubbles gently, for 45 minutes. Check occasionally to be sure the water just covers the meat. Add more if needed.

**8.** Add the salt and continue simmering for about 45 more minutes, adding water if necessary.

**9.** In a small skillet, heat 1 tablespoon of corn oil over medium heat. Have an adult help you add the flour a little at a time, stirring constantly, until the flour is completely mixed into the oil. Continue stirring the mixture for 2 to 3 minutes, until it is light brown. This mixture, called a *roux* (pronounced "roo"), is used to thicken stews or sauces.

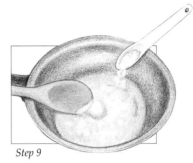
*Step 9*

**10.** Stir half of the roux into the stew and mix well. Simmer the stew, uncovered, for another 10 minutes, or until it thickens. Add the rest of the roux, if necessary, to make the stew thicker.

**11.** Spoon the stew into bowls and serve. Green chile stew goes well with tortillas. ❋

### ROASTING GREEN CHILES

*Fresh green chiles are sometimes roasted over open flames to blister the tough outer skin and make it easier to remove.*

# BIZCOCHITOS

*Bizcochitos are New Mexican sugar cookies lightly flavored with anise.*

## INGREDIENTS

¼ cup sugar
1 teaspoon cinnamon
1 cup lard or shortening
½ cup sugar
1 egg
1½ teaspoons anise
  seed
3 cups flour
1¾ teaspoons baking
  powder
½ teaspoon salt
1 teaspoon vanilla
2 tablespoons cold water,
  or as needed

*You will need an adult to help you*

## EQUIPMENT

Measuring cups
  and  spoons
Small bowl
Small spoon
Large mixing bowl
Wooden spoon
Sifter
Medium mixing bowl
Pastry cutter or fork
Rolling pin
Cookie cutters
Spatula
Cookie sheets
Potholders
Paper towels

## DIRECTIONS            *About 5 dozen cookies*

1. Preheat the oven to 375°. Combine ¼ cup sugar and cinnamon in the small bowl and set aside.

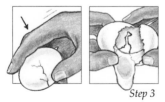
Step 2

2. Put the lard or shortening in the large mixing bowl. Use the wooden spoon to press the lard or shortening against the side of the bowl until it is soft and smooth.

Step 3

3. Mix ½ cup sugar into the lard or shortening, a little bit at a time. Stir until the mixture is light and fluffy. Then crack the egg into the mixture. Add the anise seed and mix well. Set aside.

Step 4

4. Put the sifter into the medium mixing bowl. Measure the flour, baking powder, and salt into the sifter. Then sift them into the bowl.

**5.** Add the flour mixture to the lard and sugar mixture. Use the pastry cutter or fork to cut them together until the mixture is crumbly.

*Step 5*

**6.** Add the vanilla. Then add water by teaspoons until a ball of dough forms as you stir. Use as little water as possible, enough just to hold the dough together.

**7.** Divide the dough into 3 balls. Put 2 balls of dough into the refrigerator until you are ready to use them.

**8.** Sprinkle flour onto a table or counter. Rub flour on your rolling pin to keep the dough from sticking. Roll out 1 ball of dough from the center to the edges until it is about $1/4$ inch thick.

*Step 8*

**9.** Use cookie cutters to cut out shapes. With the spatula, place the cookies on ungreased cookie sheets, about 1 inch apart.

*Step 9*

**10.** Sprinkle with the cinnamon sugar from step 1.

**11.** Bake the cookies for 10 to 12 minutes, until they are lightly browned on the bottom.

**12.** Have an adult remove the sheet from the oven. Sprinkle more of the cinnamon sugar on the cookies. Then use the spatula to move the cookies onto paper towels to cool. Continue until you have used all the dough. ✳

*Step 12*

# TAMALES

*These meat-filled **tamales** are cooked in their own cornhusk wrappers.*

## INGREDIENTS

**Filling:**
1 clove garlic
1 small onion
¾ pound pork loin
1¾ cups water
1 tablespoon corn oil
½ tablespoon flour
¼ cup ground red chiles
  (**not** chili powder)
⅜ teaspoon salt
⅛ teaspoon oregano

**Wrappers:**
4-ounce package dried
  cornhusks*

**Masa dough:**
3 cups *masa harina**
1 cup corn oil
2¼ cups water, or more
1 teaspoon salt

 *You will need an adult to help you*

## EQUIPMENT

Sharp knife
Cutting board
Small bowl
Medium baking dish
Potholders
Measuring cups
  and spoons
Large plate
Strainer
2 table forks
Large, heavy skillet
Wooden spoon
2 large mixing bowls
Large, sturdy spoon or
  powerful electric mixer
Rubber spatula
Small spoon
Steamer

*Dried cornhusks and **masa harina,** a special ground-cornmeal flour, can be found at Mexican grocery stores, and at some natural foods stores or large supermarkets.*

## DIRECTIONS    *18 to 20 tamales*

**1.** Preheat the oven to 350°.

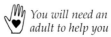
*Step 2*

**2.** To start the filling, have an adult help you peel and cut the garlic and onion. *Mince* the garlic, or cut it into tiny pieces. Put the garlic in the small bowl and set it aside. Chop the onion into medium-size pieces and put them in the baking dish.

**SACRED CORN**

*This **petroglyph**, or rock carving, shows a corn plant ready for harvesting. Corn was sacred to Josefina's Pueblo Indian neighbors—as it was to many Native Americans. According to Pueblo legend, corn was a gift from the Great Spirit. Pueblo harvest celebrations included a special Corn Dance to give thanks for the crop.*

**3.** Put the whole pork loin in the baking dish with the onion, and cover with 1¾ cups of water. Bake for about 1½ hours, or until the meat pulls apart easily.

**4.** Have an adult remove the baking dish from the oven and put the meat on a plate to cool.

**5.** Have an adult pour the pork broth through a strainer into a large measuring cup. If necessary, add water to make 1½ cups. Set the broth aside to cool.

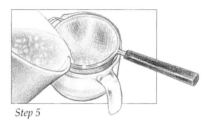

*Step 5*

**6.** When the pork is cool enough to handle, have an adult help you *shred* the meat, or pull it apart. You can use two table forks or your fingers to pull it apart into small pieces. Set the shredded meat aside.

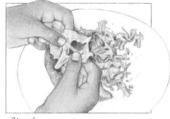

*Step 6*

**7.** In the skillet, heat the oil over medium heat, add the minced garlic and shredded pork, and stir. Add the flour, and stir constantly for about a minute as the mixture starts to brown.

*Step 7*

**8.** Stir in the pork broth, ground chiles, salt, and oregano. Mix well and let the filling *simmer*, or bubble gently, over medium heat for about 30 minutes, or until it has thickened and is almost dry. Stir often, taking care near the end of the cooking time not to burn the filling. Set it aside. ➡

*Step 8*

**9.** To prepare the cornhusk wrappers, put the dried husks into a deep bowl filled halfway with hot water. Put something heavy, such as a jar filled with water, on top of the husks to keep them underwater. After about 30 minutes, they will be soft and flexible.

*Step 10*

**10.** Gently separate the husks and rinse them under warm running water to wash away dirt, grit, or corn silk. Leave them soaking in water until you are ready to assemble the tamales.

**11.** To prepare the dough, measure the masa harina into a large mixing bowl. Add the oil, water, and salt. Mix well with a sturdy spoon or powerful electric mixer. When mixed, the masa dough should have the consistency of moist cookie dough.

*Step 12*

**12.** Lay some of the damp, softened cornhusks on the table. Tear a few of the husks into long strips, about ¼ inch wide, and lay these next to the husks. Place the filling and the masa dough on the table, making sure that everything is within reach.

*Step 13*

**13.** To assemble the tamales, lay a cornhusk flat and hold it open with 1 hand. With a rubber spatula, spread 1 to 2 tablespoons of dough in the center of the husk. Then spoon 1 to 1½ tablespoons of filling into the center of the masa dough. How much dough and filling you use will depend on the size of the husk.

**14.** Gently fold the husk in half lengthwise, so the filling is completely enclosed in the dough. Use your fingers to pat the dough to seal it. Wrap the husk snugly around the dough.

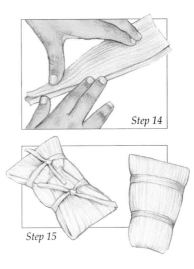

*Step 14*

**15.** Fold over the ends of the husks, and tie cornhusk strips around the ends, as shown. Set upright in the steamer basket or a bowl until ready to cook. Repeat steps 13 through 15 until all the filling and dough are used.

*Step 15*

**16.** Place the tamales on end in the steamer basket. Turn on the heat to medium and cook the tamales, covered, for 1 to 1¼ hours over *simmering*, or gently bubbling, water. When cooked, the dough is firm and no longer sticks to the cornhusk.

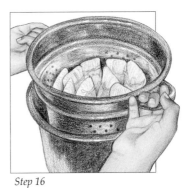

*Step 16*

**17.** Tamales should be eaten warm—but don't eat the husks! Serve the tamales with the cornhusk wrappers on, and have everyone remove and discard her own husks. ✳

*After the cornhusk wrappers are removed, spoon some red chile sauce (page 20) over your tamales.*

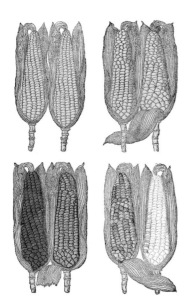

## COLORFUL CORN

*Corn comes in several different colors. For some groups of Native Americans, each color had a special significance. Blue corn was especially prized by the Pueblo Indians of northern New Mexico for its color and flavor.*

41

# PARTY IDEAS

**SAINTS**

*Spanish and Mexican settlers in New Mexico continued the Spanish tradition of making paintings and statues of saints for their homes and churches. In celebration of someone's saint's day, a painting or statue of the saint would be decorated with flowers and put in an important place in the home.*

## SPANISH NAMES

*Here are some names that were common in Josefina's time, and the feast day for each. Sometimes more than one saint has the same name, so you can pick which day to celebrate.*

**Names**

| Girls/Boys | Feast Days |
|---|---|
| Andrea/Andrés | May 21 |
| Antonia/Antonio | June 13 |
| Felipa/Felipe | May 26 |
| Francisca/Francisco | December 3 |
| Gabriela/Gabriel | March 22, 24 |
| Josefina/José | March 19 |
| Juana/Juan | May 16, June 24 |
| Juliana/Julián | March 8 |
| Luciana/Lucas | December 13 |
| Luisa/Luis | June 21 |
| Martina/Martín | November 11 |
| Micaela/Miguel | May 8 |
| Paula/Pablo | January 25, June 29 |
| Petra/Pedro | June 29 |
| Tomasa/Tomás | January 28, July 3 |

In the 1820s, there weren't parties just for children as there are today. But there were lively parties when family or friends arrived from far away. Families also celebrated religious feast days and saints' days. And people gathered when there was work that required many hands, such as husking corn, stringing chiles, or drying apples at harvest time. Whenever they gathered together, friends and neighbors shared news and gossip, played games, told stories, and sang songs.

### ✽ A NAME-DAY PARTY

When Josefina was a girl, many parents in New Mexico named their children for Catholic saints. In the Catholic Church, each saint is honored on a special day, called a *feast day*. New Mexican children celebrated their saint's day—or name day—instead of their birthday. Josefina was born on March 19, the feast day of *San José*, or Saint Joseph, so March 19 was her special day. In Josefina's time, a saint's day celebration often included music and songs, special treats like hot chocolate and fruit or pumpkin empanaditas, and small, handmade gifts.

You can have a name-day celebration, too. Pick a Spanish name from the list on this page and have a name-day celebration on the day listed. Let your guests choose Spanish names, too, and use those names during the party. Play games such as *El florón* (page 43), and serve some of the foods from this cookbook.

You can send invitations in English or Spanish, but when your guests arrive, wish all of them a warm welcome by saying *"Bienvenidos!"* (bee-EN veh-NEE-dohz)—"Welcome!"

## ❋ A HARVEST WORK PARTY

Invite some friends to a harvest work party to string apples for drying. You can buy apples at a fruit stand or store, or take your guests to pick apples at an orchard. You'll need 3 or 4 apples per person. To prepare the apples for drying, first peel, core, and cut the apples into ⅛-inch rings. Soak the rings for 15 minutes in lemon water (juice of 1 lemon per gallon of water), and then drain well. Give each guest a 1-foot piece of twine to thread through the rings. Then tie the ends together. At the end of the party, your guests can take home their strings to air-dry for several weeks until the apples are ready to eat.

As you work, sing songs and play games such as El florón, described below. Then, when the work is done, serve snacks made from some of the recipes in this cookbook.

### HARVEST FUN

*These New Mexicans are husking corn to be stored for the winter. People of all ages helped—even children. By working together, they finished big jobs faster and made the work fun. And everyone looked forward to the storytelling and songs that were an important part of working together!*

## Play El Florón

**El florón** (el flo-ROHN), or The Flower, is a guessing game. To play, choose one player to be the Guesser. Have all the other players hold their closed fists together out in front of them. While the Guesser closes her eyes, hide the florón—a flower blossom or other small object—in one of the players' hands. Say the verse below as the Guesser tries to guess who has the florón. If the Guesser is correct, the person with the florón becomes the Guesser.

> The flower goes in the hands,
> And in the hands it must be spoken.
> Guess who has it, guess who has it,
> Or be taken for a fool!

From the book *Meet Josefina*

*Josefina and her sisters husking corn.*

## MAKING MUSIC

*Much of the music enjoyed in northern New Mexico was influenced by Spanish heritage and customs.*

### Food
Bizcochitos (page 36) and pumpkin empanaditas (page 30) are good party treats. Tortillas (page 8) are easy to make or buy and can be served with sugar and cinnamon as a sweet treat. Serve hot chocolate (page 14) to drink.

### Place Settings
The Montoyas used colorful ceramic dishes from Mexico. You could use colorful paper plates and cups, even though they weren't available in Josefina's time. Or, if your parents have simple pottery dishes, ask if you can use them for your party. Put a blanket and cushions on the floor and have your guests eat sitting on the floor, as Josefina's family sometimes did.

### Decorations
Decorate with a vase of wildflowers, a pot of primroses, or a gathering of dried grasses. Place beeswax candles around the room for soft lighting.

### Clothes
Suggest that girls wear white blouses, long full skirts, and sashes. They can also wear shawls, if they have them. Boys can wear long pants and white shirts. Suggest that your guests wear moccasins, if they have them.

### Music
Spanish guitar or violin music and traditional folk music from northern New Mexico would be good background music for your party. Your librarian can help you find CDs, tapes, or records, such as recordings in the Smithsonian Folkways Series.